MAGIC
ALL AROUND

There was once a Man of Magic
who grew tired of using spells
and enchantment
to entertain people.
"Who needs to see elephants fly,
or hear pigs sing,
or meet a talking tree?"
he said to himself.
"The world is full of its own magic.
If people remembered the magic
of beautiful things,
they would not need magic wands."

The Man of Magic locked away
his jars of magic potions,
his books of wondrous spells,
and his slim, shining wand
and decided to hold a competition.
He went throughout the land, calling,
"Let it be known,
that I shall reward every person
who shows me a beautiful sight!
And to the one who shows me
the most beautiful sight of all,
I will pass on
a great and precious gift!"

Everywhere, men, women, and children
became excited.
They started looking
for the most beautiful thing
they could find.
They searched everywhere
until each had found
something beautiful.

Then they called the Man of Magic
from his wandering
and showed him wondrous things.

An astronomer took the Man of Magic
outside in the night
and showed him the stars
hanging like golden flowers
in the blackness.

A little girl opened the lid of a jar, and, together, she and the Man of Magic watched a brightly patterned butterfly wing off to freedom.

9

An old lady who grew flowers in pots showed him a velvety-red petunia, streaked in the middle.

A gardener had him look above
at the pattern of green leaves
and brown branches
against a blue, blue sky.

The Man of Magic was delighted,
and although he had locked away
much of his magic,
he still had special powers within him.
As he left the house of each person
who had shown him a beautiful sight,
the Man of Magic danced a magic step.
Behind him,
there sprang up an enchanted plant.

Friend showed friend
the things they had offered
as the most beautiful sight they could find.
They smelled the enchanted flowers
and smiled and sang
in the path of the Man of Magic.

13

A child led the Man of Magic
to a spider's web
hanging silver and perfect
in the morning.

A brown, wrinkled man
who had long ago been a sailor
showed him a wonderfully made model
of an old sailing ship.

15

Farmers took him to look on waving,
sun-baked fields of grain;
priests asked him
to look upon tall-spired churches;
children held out worn, loved toys;
mothers brought him new, pink babies;
fishermen showed him sturdy boats.
The Man of Magic
felt his heart filling with joy
and the land behind him
swelling with contentment
and happiness.

There was hardly a person in the land
who hadn't found something beautiful.

Enchanted flowers were dancing
in almost every garden
when a small boy led the Man of Magic
to his house.

"What I have to show you
is not like others have shown you,"
said the boy.
"It is not beautiful.
Some people have said
that what I am going to show you
is ugly."

From a box in the corner of the room,
the small boy picked up
a scruffy, little dog.
"Nobody wanted him
when I found him in the street,"
he said.
"His coat is patchy.
His tail is crooked,
but he's been the best friend
I've ever had,
and to me,
he's the most beautiful sight
in the world."

"Little boy," the Man of Magic said,
"since I asked the people of the land
to show me wonderful things,
instead of *me* showing *them*,
I have seen many things
of magical beauty,
but you have shown me
the most beautiful sight of all.
You know that beauty
is not always something we see,
but that it's also something we feel."

And as the Man of Magic
left the child's house,
he danced not one magic step,
not two.

He danced all around the house,
and behind him sprang up
a whole garden of enchanted flowers
that grew forever in bloom.

Then the Man of Magic left the singing, happy land
and set out for another, to remind people there
that magic is all around.